World's Best Mum
Wonderful Words

Edited by Lawrence Smith

First published in Great Britain in 2018 by:

 Young**Writers**

Young Writers
Remus House
Coltsfoot Drive
Peterborough
PE2 9BF
Telephone: 01733 890066
Website: www.youngwriters.co.uk

Printed and bound in the UK by BookPrintingUK
Website: www.bookprintinguk.com

Foreword

Here at Young Writers our defining aim
is to promote the joys of reading and writing to
children and young adults, and we are committed to
nurturing the creative talents of the next generation.
By allowing them to see their own work in print, we believe
their confidence and love of creative writing will grow.

We are proud to present this collection of poems, the
result of our latest competition 'World's Best Mum'.
Using poetry as a tool to express their appreciation and
admiration for all the things a mother does, these young
writers give personal dedications to the irreplaceable super
mum in their life. The selection process was a very difficult
task, yet the love and enthusiasm put into all of the entries
ensured that we enjoyed reading each and every one.

Including a medley of different voices and poetic styles,
such as rhyming verse and the acrostic, this is an endearing
anthology in which talented young writers use their creative
flow of words to give an important message to
their mum in a million: thank you.

To Grandma

From
Scarlett

CONTENTS

THE POEMS

MUM

My lovely mummy,
My Easter bunny,
I love you,
You love me too.
You really shine,
With such design.
You're really patient,
Like a secret agent.
You're never really serious,
You're actually quite mysterious.
You're the smartest
And a real artist.
You're all the way above
The highest of the very love.
You always do your duty,
With such beauty.
You never are really furious
And always are quite curious.
No matter how old you become,
I'll always be your little one.

Ellie Schlotterbeck

JUST LOVELY MUM

A sweet scent of roses fills the air,
Lovely cooking,
Kind and fair,
A cosy armchair fluffy and soft,
A warm heater to make you happy.

Lavenders are blue,
Roses are red,
My mum is none other than the most helpful mum in the world,
Beautiful is she.
The best mum in the world?
I think it is mine.

Susannah Potter

THE BEST MOTHER

My mother is lovely;
She always cares for me.
She loves to give me kisses in bed.
When I am sick, she would hug me, care for me and say,
"Don't worry."
However she always has a load of work to do.
She would go to work, cook at home and clean the house.
She does all of that in one day.
She really is a super heroine.
Her kindness comes from my ancestors.
They were all as sweet as honey.
This woman is extraordinary.
And I will always love her.
For she is the best mother.

Joel Choe Davies

WORLD'S BEST MUM

She is very pretty,
She is short,
She is dark,
She is kind,
She cooks food for me,
She washes me,
She washes my clothes.
She teaches me,
She cleans my home,
She goes to work every day,
She cares for me,
She helps me,
She looks after me,
I love her,
She is my mum,
World's best mum.

Sasen Amarasekara (7)

A MOTHER OR A MUM?

(Dedicated to my mum: Isobel Smart)

A mother brings you into the world
A mum is your role model
A mother feeds and clothes you
A mum helps you through the hard times and laughs with you through the good
A mother gives you a safe *house* to live in
A mum makes it a *home*
Anybody can be a mother, but it takes someone special to be a mum
My mum is my best friend xx

Abbie Smart

MUM

Mum,
You're better than all the rest.
Want to know why?
'Cause you're mine.

You're funny,
You're helpful,
You have a wonderful personality.

I'm so lucky to have you,
You're the world's best mum,
You're better than the rest,
Happy Mother's Day!

Chloe Furse

BEST MUM FOREVER

I love my mum forever
When she smiles
It makes me smile
When she laughs
It makes me laugh
My mum's heart is pure
I think it is made of gold
Thank you for comforting me
When I am upset
You are my superhero
I love you.

Sambavi Jeyasiri

BEST MUM

My mum is the best
She is not like the rest
Likes to bake
She loves cake
I hope our love will never break.

Osian Hedd Thomas-Young

MY MOTHER!

She is a shooting star,
Her eyes are chocolaty brown,
A contagious smile is always on her face,
Her voice is like a nightingale singing.
She always stays in my heart,
She fills my life with happiness,
She paints it with rainbow, sparkly lights,
She gives me her hugs and gives me her loves,
She helps me understand what's wrong or right,
Her heart is full of love,
Not even jewels can match her,
I can only give her my love.

Jahanavee Sandeep

IF YOU CAN HEAR ME, GRANDMA

If you can hear me Grandma,
Hear me from Heaven,
I just wanted to tell you something.
You were and still are probably the toughest woman I know
And yes, I have heard of Becca Swanson,
But I'm not talking about body-wise,
But on the inside.
You went through intense surgery,
Intense war.
Intense death.
So I want to tell you intensively why I love you in ten verses:
Number one: you're in charge of my mum.
Number two: you made it through.
Number three: you loved me.
Number four: you opened life's doors.
Number five: for making sure I survived.
Number six: for protecting me from my sister's silly tricks.
Number seven: for living with me in 2011.
Number eight: for managing my fate.
Number nine: for making sure I was always fine.
Number ten: because you were with me then
And you're even closer now.
You were and still are by far, the world's greatest grandma.

Muna Okorie

THE QUEEN OF ALL MOTHERS

My mum lights up the house
Without her
Life would be sad and lonely

She has a heart of gold
And love
When she touches me
I feel I can fly in the air like a dove

When I see her
She brightens up my day
She takes me everywhere I want
She is never rude or selfish to me
If I am sad she comforts and hugs me
She never ever irritates or annoys me

I love my mum
Like my bed!
This is my poem
All is said
Best mum forever!

Naithan Jeyasiri

My Mother Is The Best

My mother is really great,
She's sweet as she can be.
When I have worries she's there for me,
I pray with her before I sleep.
When I had a nightmare, she came to my room
And gave me a hug.

My mother is really caring and loving,
She's there for me when I am sick.
She sits down on my bed and gently touches my head.
When I am cold she covers me with my favourite blanket.

My mother is a very good chef.
She prepared my food that I like to eat.
She's there for me, my best teacher, when I do homework
And read my book every day.

My mother is very special to me,
that will always be remembered
As she looks after my whole life.
I should thank her for the shadow and the brightness of my
life.
I asked Jesus Christ to give her a healthy life.

Angelo Eleazar Gallaza (10)

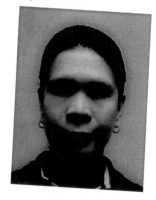

WHEN I'M OLDER...

I don't know what I'll do without you.
When we go to town,
You sometimes buy me shoes.
You make sure you kiss me goodnight
And always switch on the night light.
But that was all when I was a kid.
When I usually hide and tell a fib.

Later when I'm older,
Maybe strong and bolder,
I will suddenly leave you to go away,
Away to someone, you'll probably be grey.
I'll get a job
And during that job my head will throb.
I'll get a car,
Then I'll be driving away far to the stars.

I'll be married,
Then you'll be carried.
You'll be a grandma,
And Dad will be a grandpa.

But remember,
I'm a family member.
I'll visit you loads.
Maybe we'll cross roads.
Then again when I'm older,
The weather will probably be colder.
But when I see you, I will still come back to say,
"I love you Mum!"

Lorraine Che

SUPER MUM

My mum is super.
She can clean the house in thirty seconds flat!
I love my dad but he's not as super as my mum.
My mum says she is just as normal as you and me,
but I disagree,
Think she is a superhero,
I bet she can fly around the whole earth,
Just as fast as she can clean my room.
Today is Mother's Day and I am going to get my mum the best gift ever!
I'm going to get her a cape with 'Super Mum' on it!

Mya McEwen

MY SPECIAL NANNY

I love your squishy hugs,
When I'm sad and I'm hurting.
I love your caring heart,
When I'm alone and afraid.

I love the time you give to me,
When I know you're really busy.
But most of all...
I love you for who you are.
And that's why I call you...
My Special Nanny.

Maira Soomro

WORLD'S BEST MUM POEM

My mum is the best mum because of so many things...
She is always there for me and my sister...
She will sit up late to help me with my homework...
She never complains, even though she's always cleaning
and cooking and taking care of us...
She is always helpful...
She supports me in my netball, running up and down the
sidelines screaming like a crazy person...
My friends love her...
If I did something very wrong, she should be shouting at me,
but she listens...
If I do something that I shouldn't, she should be angry at
me, but she's calm...
She makes up her own words and somehow I know what
she's saying...
She is crazy and funny all in one...
She is the best mum in the world.

Toni Carla Van Wyk

MY MUMMY

Who is the person always kind and caring?
The person who taught me how to be sharing?
The one who was there when I was let down
And makes me tea without a frown?

The one who helps me do my homework?
The one who told me how to use my fork?
The one who walks the dog when I don't want to,
And told me the cow goes moo?
It's my mum of course, easy to guess!
Take my word, she's no mess.
She may not be what others seek,
But in my eyes she's unique.

Natalia Lipowska (10)

MY MUMMY!

I will love you for a thousand years,
Because you always wipe away my tears.
You always put me first
And look after me like a nurse.

Without you I would be lost,
I can never replace you at any cost.
You make me so, so happy
And thank you for always changing my nappy!

Meraj Soomro

I LOVE YOU, MUMMY

I love you, Mummy,
I really do.
You care for me,
I care for you,
Me and you,
We make a two.
I love you, Mummy,
I really do.
You buy me my favourite mag,
You care when I'm struggling with my spag,
When I fall down,
You will turn it around,
Put my feet on the ground,
I know you work hard to give me food,
I would count you as my best dude.
Because I love you Mummy, I really do,
Me and you we'll stick like glue.

Antonia Boevska

MY MOTHER

My mum, a loving and wonderful mum,
Looking out for me so I'm not so dumb,
She's kind caring and so much more
And intelligent and clever, that's for sure.

And sometimes when I'm upset and sad,
My mother helps me and I am glad,
To say that's my mum, sat on that chair
And I know, no matter where I am, she is always there.

If it weren't for my mum, who's always here for me,
I wouldn't see my friends, play games or see the sea,
So, I'm happy that you do all of this for us,
Me and my brothers, of whom you make such a fuss.

One day I wish to be just like you,
Caring, intelligent and kind too,
I really hope you are always here for me,
Best friends forever, we will always be!

Elizabeth Codner

HERO

My mum's the best
I definitely know
When I'm hurt
She helps me out
When I'm bored
She's willing to play a game
When I'm hungry
She's the chef
When I want a story
She's the one to read it
My mum's the best
I definitely know
She's a... hero!

Naomi Francis (8)

Best Mummy

B eing so kind
E xcellent cooking
S pecial like a diamond
T o the best mummy

M ummy, you are so caring
U nique like a star
M y shining star
M agnificent you are
Y ou are always here when I need you.

Elizabeth Young

WORLD'S BEST MUM POEM

No matter how far... She is always my mum
No matter where... She is always my mum
No matter where I am or how far away...
I am her daughter and she is my mummy

My mum in a million or even a trillion, my number one
If I'm ill she will always be there with every single care
To hold my hand or stroke my hair

Mum I want to let you know that however far you go
You are always in my heart and always very smart
My mum in a hundred, million, billion, trillion.

Lauren Symonds

Mommy

I love my mum!
I think my mum is the best mum!
Here's why,
She is as sweet as pie,
She helps me study,
She gives me time,
She gives me food,
She plays with me,
She cares for me,
She is always happy with me,
She talks to me,
She comforts me,
She lets me experience my childhood,
I am proud of her!

Afifah Ahmed Arpita (9)

WORLD'S BEST MUM

My mummy obeys the true God
And doesn't make him mad
She loves him with all her might
And God never gets sad

Mummy also loves me
And also she always looks nice
And sometimes I can help her
I think more than twice.

Femi Soyoye (9)

BEST MUMMY EVER

Best mummy ever
You've been cooking for me
And going to the shop to buy food for me
And working at your school
And the best parts of all parts
Are working with me
So you Mummy
Get the best mother's break of fun!

Ayo Soyoye

A World In Love

In every religion love means the same, your mother comes first,
You are the reason for her happiness and for her sorrow.
Don't be the reason for her tears,
Be the reason behind her smile.
Paradise lies beneath your mother's feet.
Always greet her and look after her.
Take her blessings and you will always succeed.
If you're happy so your mother is too.
As a mother's heart beats for her children.
Money doesn't buy your mother's love, you do,
Celebrate every day with your mother, not only Mother's Day.

Syeda Sameena Begum (12)

My Mummy

M y mummy is better than the rest
Y outhful are her looks

M other's Day is her favourite
U nderneath her beauty is love
M y mummy is always kind
M y mummy will never embarrass me
 Y ou don't need a present, all she needs is you!

She is the most amazing person in the world!

Zara Dorman

THE VERY BEST

My mum is the best,
She never takes a single rest,
My mum is so cool,
She takes us to the swimming pool.

My mum is a great cook,
She doesn't need a recipe book.
My mum is the very best,
She most definitely beats the rest!

Clemmie Davies

THE VERY BEST

My mum is the best,
She never takes a single rest,
My mum is so cool,
She takes us to the swimming pool.

My mum is a great cook,
She doesn't need a recipe book.
My mum is the very best,
She most definitely beats the rest!

Bobby Davies

DEAR MUM

You are so funny

That I can't believe
How funny you are

You are so nice that
I cannot live without you.
I love you so much!

Sacha Imankerdjo-Lambert

MY MOTHER

In my bedroom you're a storyteller,
In the kitchen you are a chef,
At work you are the doctor,
When do you rest?

With my homework you're a mathematician,
With the house you are the maid,
With the neighbours you are a friend,
You are worth more than anyone can pay.

At the pool you're a lifeguard,
In all sports a player too,
At home you are a linguist,
There is nothing you can't do.

When I am sad you are a comedian,
Any special event that I am in you're there all the time,
Anywhere, anytime, where I want to go,
You'll take me there no matter what.

Lara Prabhu-Desai (9)

YOU ARE ONE IN A MILLION

You've helped me through my darkest days
And got me through things I thought were impossible,
You made me smile when I thought I couldn't
And showed me love when I was scared,
You are one in a million.

You gave me independence but never left my side,
And helped me make memories that will last forever,
You were the parent who was always there
And showed me what it looked like to really care,
You are one in a million.

You made me feel safe when I felt alone
And you are always there to listen,
You turned our house into a home
And gave me a friend who will never leave,
You are one in a million.

You picked me up when I was down
And showed me how to be the real me
You taught me that I do matter
And these are just some of the reasons why,
You are one in a million.
But most of all I'm proud to call you Mum.
I love you.

Tawney Revell

My Mad Mum!

I'd say that my mum was perfect,
Or that she never groans,
But to do that would be lying,
Right down till the bones.

I'd say that she never grumbles,
But that would not be true;
For she sometimes does get angry,
As mothers often do.

My mother may be silly,
Or embarrassing at times,
But she has always been there for me and my brother,
Through all of our lives.

And although she may have her imperfections
And she might not come out on top,
For me she will forever be the best
And that will never stop.

And although we make each other angry
And think each other a pain,
Our love for each other will never stop
And that will stay the same.

Lizzie Poulson

MY MOST MAGNIFICENT MUM

Best mum in the world,
The one who understands.
For she is always giving and forgiving
And considers her kids her base of living.

Mum loves me all the time,
Even when I am a pest,
She always takes good care of me,
My mother is the best.

I know that my mother is really the best,
So I say to myself, "I'm sure I'm blessed."
In my heart are many memories,
Of the loving things you've done
And today I want to tell you,
That I'm thankful for each one.

My mother, so dear,
Throughout my life you're always near.
A tender smile to guide my way,
You're the sunshine to light my day.

Here's a simple poem,
Straight from my heart,
I love you, Mum
And that's a start!

Sihaam Bazi Ahmed

MY MUM

My mum's the best
She hardly ever shouts
She's better than the rest
Because she's always about

I know you all think highly
Of your mothers too
But at least your brothers
Don't act like a walking zoo

So yes, my mother's great
She really is fantastic
She doesn't ever deflate
It's like she runs on static.

My mum is the best
And she always will be.
Happy Mother's Day.

Mckenzie Anderson (13)

MY MUM

You always seem to know what's wrong,
Before I even say,
You seem to know what's on my mind,
Or if I'm down that day.

I never have to ask for help,
You're always there to guide me,
If at times I need support,
You're always right beside me,

You've been my rock throughout my life,
Wanting nothing in return,
You've made me who I am today,
Helping me to grow and learn.

Thank you will never be enough,
For all the things you've done,
You're my friend, my counsellor,
My guardian angel,
But most importantly,
My mum.

Jaycie Kabir

BEST MUM

You're always there to understand,
To listen, to lend a hand,
You are a tree I lean upon,
You never leave me alone.

You're the sunlight in my day,
You are the moon that gazes from far away,
You are my friend,
You never end.

You are the one who knows me best,
You can tell me from the rest,
You are the sturdy oak, a beam,
The defender of our team.

You keep my smile on my face
And you make me happy all days,
You are my love, my life, my mum,
Your heart is bigger than a plum.

The rock that's there whatever the weather,
You keep our family together

The best mum is my mum,
I love you, Mum!

Elif Aptula

ROOM IN HER HEART

The best thing is here,
Her name is Mummy,
Although her name is new to the world,
I think it's perfect for her,
She may be daft, silly and funny,
She still has room in her heart,
For all of her children and the whole family,
So if you feel down you know where to come!

Beatrice-Alice Taylor-Fullwood (9)

FOR YOU ON MOTHER'S DAY

I love you so much Mum,
There's something about you that's very special,
Why do people treat others badly but not you,
You help me when I'm down,
You make me laugh,
Sometimes you make me laugh that much I cry,
You push me on to do a lot of things in my life,
That's why you are the best mum in the world,
I'm making you number one in life.

Jasmine Sproat (14)

THE ONE AND ONLY MUM!

"You only get one mum,
so look after her," I get told.
They are special like treasure or gold.

I've got an amazing mum,
She's always happy, unlike some!
Kisses and hugs are always there,
I suppose she's like a warm friendly bear!

We can always have a good laugh,
When you think about it,
She's the cow and I'm the calf!

I love baking with her,
"Now get the spoon and stir, stir, stir!"
She will say as the blender begins to whir!

You're never too old to be read to at night,
Every day she tucks me up nice and tight!

When homework gets tough and I give a loud huff,
She says let me see what you've got to do,
Then has a look and says it's over to you!

Mums are brilliant, mums are fun,
But remember, you only get one!

Isabel Arrowsmith (12)

MY MUMMY IS THE BEST!

My mum is my life,
She is sharper than a knife,
She never lets us down,
So she needs a crown.

I know she is my mummy,
Because I was born from her tummy.
Mummy is the best,
Because she doesn't need a test.

She has an enormous power
And she is taller than a tower.
Nobody is better than her,
So they would have to try again.

She needs a treat,
Because she is always neat.
I care for you,
Because each day will be new.

Miracle Onyedikachukwu Anosike

MY MAGIC MOTHER

Hi Mother over here
My face lights up when you are near
Driving your big blue car over to school
If I didn't have you I'd be a failing fool

Doing jobs all around the house
Making the tea and running the bath
If I had to do it
I'd go mad like a psychopath

Mowing the yard every day
I've tried to do it but it just stays
I may not be as strong as a wrestler
But I just need to say I love you forever

Marvellous majestic and magic too
These are the things I love about you
Treating me more than any other
My face still lights up my beautiful mother
Happy Mother's Day, Mum.

Britton Lee Alan Kolka

WORLD'S BEST MOM

(A Kennings Poem)

My mum is a:
Heart-warmer,
Issue-handler,
Hard worker,
Thorough laugher,
Mind-reader,
Food-supplier,
Time-keeper,
Passion-seeker,
Magazine lover,
Encouraging fighter,
But most of all she is the best mum!

Juriel Owusu (10)

LOVE YOU, MUM!

My mother is
My friend so dear.
Throughout my life
You're always here.
You're always trying
To guide my way.
You're the sunshine
To light my day.
I love you, Mum,
Always and forever!

Aksa Ahmed (11)

WORLD'S BEST MUM

Mum is the best,
She's the greatest mum in the west,
She's a game-player,
She's a bug-slayer,
She always cooks tea,
She's married to Lee.

I will love her forever,
I will forget her never.
If there is a school event, she'll attend,
My love for her will never end.
She never looks glum,
I really love my mum.

Scarlett Boardman

THANK YOU MUMMY!

Thank you Mummy for all that you do,
Thank you for making my dreams come true,
Thank you for working to get everything I need,
I think you are very beautiful indeed,
I hope one day I can be like you,
When my family are growing, young and new,
So I would like to remind you of how I love you,
Thank you Mummy for all that you do.

Olivia Maynard (10)

HOW MUCH I LOVE MY MUM!

As vast as the ocean,
As big as the sea,
My love for you is irreplaceable!

You help with hard homework
And spellings too,
Terrible year six maths,
You mostly know what to do!

Baking or dancing,
Skating or swimming,
You support me whatever I do,
Even if you need to rush.

You spend time with me,
When I feel down
And take me out shopping,
Into town!

Thank you so much for being my mum,
Even though there is no choice,
I'm sad to say this poem is done,
I just want to say,
I love you!

Mia Mancari

FOR YOU, WHO KEEPS ME GOING

You shine up the stars,
You light up my heart,
Even if sometimes we have wars,
We always forget it to have a new start.

I know when I'm with you,
I can start brand new,
Because you are the one,
The one that has always been there.

Who is going to catch me when I fall?
I know it's going to be you, even if you don't hear my call,
Because you are my wall,
My walls that keep me standing,
You are my mum.

Jappreet Kaur

MY KIND OF SUPERHERO

My kind of superhero isn't famous,
She isn't in any kind of movie
She isn't plastered on any type of poster
My kind of superhero has a loving smile, a gigantic heart
My superhero gives warm, confiding hugs, words of wisdom
along with soft kisses
My kind of superhero raised me all by herself,
My superhero is strong and proud,
She fills me with courage.
My superhero isn't good at jokes but she still makes me
laugh,
My superhero is my mum
And she's the most motivating superhero I could ever be
inspired by.

Sian Suzanne Bonnici

MY MOTHER IS THE BEST

M y mother is the best of all the rest,
O rganised is she, to juggle everything around me,
T hough she is strict, I love her the most,
H er hugs and kisses are as sweet as fructose.
E ven hard quizzes she can win easily,
R igorous is she, with everything.

Mother, mother, mother as I hear from all,
Mother, mother, mother created by God as he couldn't be
everywhere.

Shivani Patel

MUMMY

M y
U nique
M um.

Everything you have done for me is so special,
My magic, marvellous mum is the best mum in the whole wide world,
She magics my frowns away and dries up my tears,
She always thinks of me and helps me when I'm stuck,
So that is why my mummy is

M agic,
U nique and
M arvellous.

Phoebe Corley

Yummy Mummy

M y mummy is a yummy mummy
U nbelievably kind is my mummy
M y mummy is loving
M y mummy is caring
Y ou know my mummy is the best mummy ever!

Aaria Bains

I CAN'T LIVE WITHOUT YOU

There for me when I fall,
You stand above them all,
No matter what it is,
What I can't live without,
Is you.

With you I am not afraid,
Even on the darkest of days,
Alone I am not,
Because you are there on the spot.

Here today,
Do not be dismayed,
This is the time to celebrate with you.

You are the best,
I am luckier than the rest,
To have you,
Have a good time,
Do not be surprised,
If you get the greatest award of them all.

There is one person I can't live without,
That is you,
Yourself!

Mathilda Peters

KOCHANEJ MAMIE (TO MY LOVELY MUM)

It's your day today
And I think it should be every day
So here I am shouting:

Hip hip hooray!
I love you!
Thank you for looking after me every day!

For waking me up every morning
And tucking me back into bed at the end of the day,

For my lovely, shiny, plaited hair
And my school uniform that smells like fresh air.

For all the kisses and hugs, even when I feel grumpy,
You never say, "No, not now, I am tired..."
And with your lovely smile,
You are always there by my side.

So today put your feet up
And I will make you cup of tea,
To say how much you mean to me,
Happy Mother's Day!

Emily Agha Mohammad Zadeh

MY MARVELLOUS MUM

The world's best mum
Can you guess who she is
Well let me give you a hint
But try not to squint.

She knows when something's wrong
And she seems to read my mind
Or even when I'm down
She's always there for me.

She's busy as a bee
Shiny as a diamond
Smart as a calculator
And brave as an alligator.

Thank you is not enough
For all of what she has done
She's my friend, teacher, doctor
And most importantly she's my mum!

Nour Mohamed Elshirazy

MY MUM!

My mum is the most wonderful person in the world.
What can I do without you Mum!
She helps me every day,
She cooks for my family,
She looks after me when I'm sick,
She makes me happy when I'm sad,
She helps me with my homework,
She teaches me to follow in my faith,
She takes me to school,
She watches my dance shows, music shows,
She gives me hugs and kisses every day.
What can I do without you Mum!
I can't say anymore but all I'm trying to say,
Is that she does so much for me,
So she's the number one mum in the world!

Londeka Siphosethu Gcaba (8)

To My Beloved Mum!

Mum, Mummy, Mother,
Whatever you want it to be,
They are all very precious and not just to me!
Oh look there! It's mother Diana Lou!
Oh look! There's your mum too!
They are always very kind,
Mum, I love you!
Keep your love deep inside,
Always in your heart,
So what if you're very old,
We will never break apart!
Of course I love Dad
And dear brother too,
But this poem is just for you!
Happy Mother's Day!

Danielle Jaedian Villegas Veluz

58

Mum

My mum is special,
She gives me warm hugs,
She is the best mum ever.
She is as soft as a cat.
She is a good cook.
I love my mum and she loves me.

Habeeba Ahmed

MY MUM

M other's Day is coming up!
Y ay, I can get her lots of presents!

M y mum is the queen of Mother's Day!
U nique, amazing, beautiful; my mum is all of these!
M y mum's the best mum in the universe!

Mia Nicholls

YOU ARE MY HEART AND SOUL

Thank you...
For standing by me through thick and thin,
For not giving up on me when I didn't win,
For your patience when I kept pushing you away,
For caring when I said I didn't need you anyway.

I am grateful knowing...
I can count on your strength,
Ask for your support and know you'll go to any length,
When I lose my way,
You help me get back on track,
When in pain,
Your comfort soothes and brings me back.

I am lucky because...
When I was sad you gave me faith and hope,
When I was confused you taught me how to cope,
When I felt I couldn't go on,
You carried me for long miles
When I didn't believe,
You restored my smiles.

Mum, thank you...
For your guidance and the faith you've shown,
For giving me a safe place where I have grown,
For showing me how to strive,
Because of your love
I will survive.

Beth Anderson

MUM

Mum,
You welcome me home, when I've had a bad day,
The love you fill me with, in words I can't say,
Your endless care, could fill forever,
My happiness will not ever stop, never.

Mum,
You help me with every small step I make,
No matter what it is and how long it takes,
Pushing me hard to help me get through,
I really don't know, what I'd do without you.

Mum,
You welcome me home, when I've had a bad day,
The love you fill with me, in words I can't say,
Your endless care, could fill forever,
My happiness will not ever stop, never.

Mum,
You work so hard every single day,
Your painted artwork perfectly made,
Our house is always tidy because of you,
At the end of the day, you see us all through.

Mum,
You welcome me home, when I've had a bad day,
The love you fill me with, in words I can't say,
Your endless care, could fill forever,
My happiness will not ever stop, never.

Mum,
You are special.

Jack Beales

SUPER MUMMY

My mummy is the best,
She's always on the go,
And rarely gets to rest,
She wakes me up every day.
With hugs and kisses
And lots to say.
She helps me get ready
And makes my breakfast.
She even cleans up,
Leaving not a crust.
She used to work full time
And came home very late,
But now she's left
And picks me up every day outside the school gate.
We have lots of fun together
And I will love my mummy forever and ever.

Simar Kaur Bharya (9)

My Mum

My mum is so special,
She makes lots of things using the kettle,
My mum helps and supports me
And is hard working as you can see.

My mum guides me on to the right path
And she used to help me have a bath.
My mum loves me so much that the love can't even fit in a cart,
She may not always be with me physically,
But she is always with me in my heart.

My mum says, "I love you,"
I say, "I love you too,"
My mum and I love each other,
I am very glad that she is my mother.

My mum is the world's best mum,
She likes chewing gum.
Mum, I dedicate this to you,
You love me and I love you.

Irza Tariq (10)

My Marvellous Mum

Thank you Mum for all your love,
That you have forever showered upon me from above,
You always shine like the brightest star every day,
Helping to light my very way!

Your wonderful love is beyond all measures,
So you should always be treated like the world's best treasures,
Whenever I am down you bring my spirit up
And banish all darkness into an empty cup!

Always remember that you are close to my heart
And we will never be far apart,
Your hugs are the best anyone could wish for,
As they come from your sweet, inner core.

You allow for my dreams to be fulfilled,
Which makes me proud and strong willed,
So now is the time to make my call,
To give you the greatest thanks of all.

Lily Rutterford

DISTINCTIVE MUM

To me, my mum is the best,
She's better than all the rest,
She gives me cuddles when I need them most,
She cooks the very best roasts!

She's got silky brown hair
And I've luckily inherited her sapphire blue eyes,
She treats us on the very best holidays,
That's why she's the best,
Better than all the rest.

Thanks Mum,
For always looking over me,
Watching me grow up.

Charlotte Beaumont

BEST MUM

Mum is amazing, Mum is my hero,
Mum is faster than an aeroplane can fly,
Mummy has juicy apples, Mum makes the best apple pie.
I love my mum more than the stars,
My mum I love more than anything.
My mum is the best because she always brings my scooter,
Best mum... My mum!

Chloé Georgia Kaspersen

MUM'S THE WORD

She's always there when I wake up,
When I come home from school and when I got to sleep.
She is always busy but makes time for me.
She keeps my room tidy, even when it's a slag heap.

She works day and night and makes everything perfect.
She wakes me up when I oversleep.
She may sometimes get angry,
But I know that the mountain of her love is indubitably steep.

Rayna Sunny

DEAR MOTHER

Dear Mother,
I have never had a brother,
Nor a sister but you still spoil me rotten
And tell me off when I'm bad
And make me learn my lesson
Like all mothers should do,
But this is my mum, the one I love and care for.
Even though I shout at you all the time when I'm mad,
You never give up with me
And I love you for that.
You have never not answered the call
And ended it without saying I love you,
But this is what mother means to me.

M y mother forever and always,
O n my side no matter what,
T hank you for being there,
H elping me through tough times.
E ver not picked up the call? No.
R ight when I'm wrong but says I'm right, even though I'm
   not.

Fay Elizabeth Herbert

MY MUM

My mum's my mum, my mum's my dad.
She's the best mum I could've ever had.
My mum's my mam, my my mum's my mate.
She's a dysfunctional lady, she's always late.

My mum's my mother, my mum's the queen.
She wishes for but doesn't get a house that's squeaky clean.
My mum's my ma, my mum's my teacher
And when there's a mess, she's the loudest preacher.

My mum's my mummy, my mum's my hero.
She's different from the other moms, she won't settle for zero.
My mum's not just a parent, my mum's my world.
Her hair is crimson red but you'll never see it curled.

Happy Mother's Day.

Kane Whitehouse (15)

BEST MUM EVER!

When you wake up, their smiling face is there,
Along with lots of happiness which they like to share.
Then you might get dressed and go downstairs,
You're lucky to have your mum there.
They go off to work and work hard for you,
Tell them you're grateful, that's what you should do.
They then come home, smiling once more
And might help you with homework, you love them for sure.
Everything I have is because of my mummy,
She makes my world seem bright and happy and sunny.
My mum is the loveliest person I could ever meet,
Her parenting skills are so very chic.
I'm so very grateful for all that you've done,
You make my world bright and full of fun.
Mummy you are the best person ever,
I love you so much and will do forever!

Chloe Armstrong

THANK YOU FOR BEING MY MUM

I love all her hugs and kisses,
I love all her funny jokes,
I love my mum for always being there for me,
When I needed her the most.
I thank my mum for all the crazy stuff she does for me,
I thank my mum for all the times she's had to put up with my yapping.
I love all my mum's delicious cooking,
Pasties, roast chicken, curry, etcetera,
Thank you for being my mum,
I love you my mum,
I love my mum,
Thank you.

Kelsey Rickard

MY MUM

My mum is my favourite person
She makes my days so bright
Her silly jokes and terrible eyesight
Keep me laughing all through the day and night
She forgets what she's doing, loses direction and never
remembers the time!
But if I ever needed a hug, a smile or a "Are you okay?"
My mum is first in line
She teaches me what's right
To be strong, to be true and so kind
I keep these lessons close to my heart
Because my mum is always in mine.

Eirinn Whelan

My Mum

My mum always helps me,
When I am stuck,
She's as kind as a queen
And as naughty as Puck.
I feel like I'm flying,
When I hold her hand.
She smells of roses, cinnamon, berries and...
... she has glorious hugs, as good as chocolate.

Lara Stockley

THE WORLD'S GREATEST MUM

Some call her mum, some call her mummy
She can be embarrassing and also kind of funny
My mum's better than all the rest
In every single way she is just the best!

In my opinion I have the world's greatest mum
Because in my eyes she is as bright as the sun
I feel like she is super special
I always see her calm and she is always about to settle.

My mum offers love and comfort
So in my heart I always need to love her
Not a day goes by that she is not in my heart
There would be a kiss and a cuddle every day on a chart.

I don't know how but she always has spare time
No one can ever cross her patience line
Making this poem I think I'm safe to say
I have the best mum in the world, every single day.

Ben Buchanan (11)

WONDERFUL MUM

I am blessed with a wonderful mum,
Who makes sure that I am never glum,
She makes delicious, delectable food,
To which I am delightfully glued.

When I am in need,
She always supports me, indeed,
A pillar, on whom I lean a lot,
When I encounter something tricky to concoct.

She's just not only helpful,
More than that, resourceful.
My mum: a wonder filled with kindness,
A description of words is way too less.

Sahana Sakthivel (7)

My Best Mummy

M y mummy is the very best,
Y es, she is and I am blessed!

M ummy always takes me to school,
U nless it's the holidays and that is cool.
M y mummy always gives me a snack,
M mm, my favourite is flapjack!
Y es, my mummy is the best...

I think she beats the rest.
S he tidies and cleans and looks after me...

T hen after school, she cooks my tea.
H er eyes are beautiful and her smile too,
E ven when she cleans the loo!

B est friends are what we are,
E verywhere we go, near or far.
S he gives me cuddles every day.
T hank you Mummy is what I'm trying to say!

Millie Ava Jade Robinson

MY MUM IS GREAT

M ummy, Mummy you're so funny I love you so much.
Y es Mummy, I've had a shower, now you have one too.

M y mum is awesome, I love you so much.
U nder the stars lie you and me chatting and loving each other.
M y mum is the greatest out of them all, even big and small.

I nside our house lives you, the mum I'd love most.
S uper, I get to spend the day with you alone.

G rabbing your hand I said, "I love you Mummy."
R eading a book with you would be a pleasure,
E ating cookies with you is so fun but a tiny bit cheeky.
A fter tea I read my book to you, I love you.
T ime for bed, sorry to say, yay, you're taking me up. We say, "I love you!"

Keira Ford

LOVE ALWAYS

Mummy, you're the best
Your inspiration is true
I love you millions
And thank you for being you
And for everything you do
So here's a happy Mother's Day wish just for you
Love you always.

Chanelle Frankie Russo

THE GREATEST GIFT

Who cares for us and guides us?
You can feel their love and gentleness
As they walk through life beside us.

They do great things for us every day
They whisper in our ears
They even hold us in their arms
When we are filled with fears.

They are always there to give us a hug
And try to make us smile
They treat us with respect and love
They go that extra mile.

God blessed me with an angel
I'm proud to call my own
She's been with me through life
She's been with me as I've grown.

She's guided me the best she could
She's taught me like no other
And I'm thankful I'm the lucky one who gets to call her
mother.

A mother gives her children stepping stones to the stars
Her love is unconditional
Her heart has no bars.

A mother teaches her children to be confident and bold
Her special love to her children
Is more valuable than gold.

A mum is the one who understands
The things you do and say
The one who overlooks your faults
And sees the best in you.

80

A mum is one whose special love inspires you day by day
Who fills your heart with gladness
In a warm and thoughtful way
A mother is these great things and more
The greatest treasure known

And the greatest mother in all of the world
Is the one I call my own.
Happy Mother's Day!

Libby Thornton

BEST MUM EVER!

My mum is one of a kind,
Offering kindness and pure love.
For she is the best,
I fly like a dove.

She believes in me,
She's the rock that I stand on.
Always supportive,
A mum I can rely on.

I truly love my mum,
Whom I will always remember,
My favourite person,
A unique emblem.

Jesciel Clare Telan

MUMS ARE INCREDIBLE

I love my mum,
My mum loves me,
Mums are cool, don't you see?
She is never feeling down
And never wears a frown,
Love is what we share
A mass of kindness and care
She is kind and sweet,
To everyone she meets,
She shares her time, just for me,
Mums are so busy don't you see,
She fills her heart with love and care,
Each possession she owns, she loves to share,
My mum supports me,
She loves what I do,
Mums are incredible, don't you see!
I love her in every way,
I love hearing anything she has to say
But for all the special things mums do,
I just need to say,
I love you!

Ruby Hall

WORLD'S BEST MUM

I will always love you
For ever you will be my mum
If I had to pick between anyone in the world
I would pick you

You are so loving and caring
You would give up anything for me
And that will always be

You love me and I love you
That will never change
No matter what you do

I love the way you call me sweetheart
I love how you cook
I also love when you read me a book

I feel so nice when I'm around you
You are the world's best mum.

Nisa Krasniqi (8)

Mummy Equals Me

When you tell me to go and do my work this is what my
work is.
Mum, mummy, mother, best friend, my doctor,
My nurse, my teddy bear, my dreams in a jar,
My chef, my carer, my hair styler, my teacher
And my infinity love. I cannot live without your love.
One day I dream to be just like you.
Caring, loving, strong and brave.
You taught me to always give and not take,
You taught me to always look after the less fortunate.
I love it most when you hug me,
I feel safe and warm.
Mummy equals me.
I equal Mummy.
I love my mummy, I love my mummy.
One day when I am big and you are a granny,
I will look after you like you look after me,
I love my mummy, I love my mummy, I love my mummy.

Sidrah Ali (6)

THE WORLD'S BEST MUM

I love you Mum,
You're the best,
You are better,
Than all the rest.

You make me food,
You give me hugs,
You clean my room,
And all the house.

You're really funny,
I love the jokes you tell,
About Daddy's tummy.

I love you more than anything in the world,
You are officially,
The world's best mum!

Sachal Salman

My Mum Is A Superhero

Oh, look who comes flying through the skies with her cape up high?
Is it a fly?
No, it's my mum flying up high.
She swoops down and grabs me, taking me up high to the skies, where birds fly.
She takes me through a cloud with no doubt.
She tells me how she went out into the universe and had tea with Superman,
Then we come home and I know my mum's the best,
because she beats the rest.
My mum is special out of all the others in every way because our love is invincible and she always listens to my problems.

Aron Peter Arkosi

MOTHER'S DAY

Sweet, sweet mum,
Thank you for the things you've done.
Thank you for cooking my tea on Saturday and Sunday too,
But most of all I love you!
All the things you've done,
Have made me so happy,
Thank you! I love you!

Isabella Owen

My Mum!

I love my mum
She is lots of fun
My mum is kind and friendly
When I grow up I want to be just like her
She has nice dark skin and long black hair
My mum is very funny
She goes to work and makes lots of money
My mum is better than all the rest!

Lacie-Mai Wharton

MY GREAT MUM

M ummy is the best mum ever,
U ltimate hugs, full of love,
M agnificent personality,
M ost loving person ever,
Y ummy food by my mum.

Cian Hempenstall

I Love Mummy and Gegor

M ummy is the best,
U nbelievable love,
M agical heart,
M ummy is a mermaid,
Y ou are very nice.

G egor is a flower.
E xcellent at everything.
G reat at tricky questions.
O ur family loves you.
R emember you're the best grandma.

Daisy Hempenstall

MY MUMMY

M arvellous mummy,
U nited together,
M agical girl,
M ost kind mummy,
Y ou are the best.

Ava Hempenstall

Mother's Day Poem

M y mummy's like a moon flower, so pretty and so graceful.
U tterly an umbrella plant, to protect me from harm.
M y mummy's like a Muscari, so aware and so watchful.
M y mummy's like a Meconopsis, so kind and gentle.
Y es, mummy's like a yellow archangel, my guardian angel!

Amelie Jane Marianne Junkison

THE FIRE OF MY CANDLE

Awake in the dark where there's only fear,
In a room a candle appears,
It's not warm but cold and all alone,
No love and never a light to spare,
Until you came and showed it love,
Until you came no love was there.
Then all of a sudden a light flickers then a fire appears,
A fire of warmth and welcoming light.
If it wasn't for you, no light would be there,
If it wasn't for you, no love in the air.
You are the fire, the fire that lights a sad, lonely and afraid candle,
Into a bright, happy fearless candle,
Who spreads its love, like you once did to me.

Theo O'Connor

AMAZING MUMMY

My mummy is my best friend
I really cannot pretend
My mummy is my angel
She sat there on the table

My mummy is my helper
Always giving me shelter
My mummy is my teacher
I say, a beautiful creature

My mummy is my food maker
So I must never shake her
My mummy is a nurse
She has money in her purse

My mummy is amazing
She works hard child raising
So I say thank you mummy
You're just amazing.

Jasmine Leila Schwartz

MY MOTHER'S DAY POEM

Mummy, Mother, Mum;
Doesn't matter what I call you,
Out of space, around the world,
That's how much I love you.

Always by my side,
Supporting me along the way,
Education, school,
Kissing me every single day,
I know it's hard, so...
Put your feet up, rest and relax,
You deserve a day like this.

Roses, tulips, daisies too,
Breakfast in bed, I know you're fed up,
But you're our queen for the day,
And presents, kisses and hugs for you.

Round the universe I'll go,
Shouting, "Claire, you're the world's best mum,
I love you!"

Amelia Grace Mullaney

My Ideal Mum!

My mum is the one I love,
The one I cuddle,
The one I kiss.

My mum is the one who laughs,
The one who cooks,
The one who cares.

My mum is the nicest mum,
The cuddliest mum,
The funniest mum.

My mum is the one who loves,
The one who smiles,
The one who tucks me up for bed.

My mum is the only one that gives me treats,
The only one that snuggles up,
The only one that watches TV with me.
In other words: my mum is everything!

Jessica Rose Hale

THE BEST MUM IN THE WORLD

Mum, what can I say?
It's always my special day
So now for a change, here's your gift
A special, little daughter lift
From me
To my mum, the best
I get home, there is my tea
You are my revising partner for every test
Yet what do you get?
A handful of dirty socks
That makes you feel like you are being mocked
So now it is my chance to say
Well thanks!
'Cause whatever you do
Whether it is cleaning my shoe
Or combing my hair
You do it with care
Come to think of it, it doesn't seem fair
So I just want you know
I do love you
So Happy Mother's Day
And thanks for all the wonderful things you do for me!

Emily Barrett

Best Mum

My mum is the best,
Better than the rest,
Every day it's a feast.
She takes care of me,
I can't bear to say she isn't my mum.

She's my mummy,
My tummy is always full,
Yummy in my tummy.
She clothes me every day,
She is the best of them all.

Her love is unstoppable,
I love her above and below.
I will love her till I die,
When I am ill she takes care of me,
Even if she becomes ill, she will still look after me.

She never gives up on me,
Yup, she's my mum.
She is always there for me

I swear she's my mum,
'Cause she is!

Leeza Mariam Siddique

MY WONDERFUL FOSTER MUM

Wendy, I am so lucky to have you in my life.
You offer me good advice and teach me so many things,
About how to get through my daily life.
You have been there for me since I came to live with you.
You help me through upsetting moments
And when I needed somebody the most.
Sometimes we might argue but I know that in the end,
You're always there for me

M is for making me feel happy and making me feel safe.
O is for offering me help when I needed it the most.
T is for teaching me many things that I didn't even know.
H is for helping me throughout my life.
E is for everything you do for me.
R is for a really special foster mum like you.

Even when I release a tear she replaces it with a smile,
I miss my mum very deeply because I haven't seen her for a long while,
But my foster mum isn't just a temporary placement,
She will have a place in my heart forever and ever,
Even when I encounter my real mum when I am older.
Thank you for loving me as your own.
I'd say you deserve a happy Mother's Day poem,
For a loving and caring foster mum like you.

Angel Gabbott (15)

You're A Mum In A Million

My mum is the number one mum,
She can knock down all the rest,
She's top of the leader board,
But she never has a rest.

My mum is the number one mum,
She is certainly not dumb,
She's gonna get the cup,
Thank you for being the best mum.
You're a mum in a million.

Lauren Elizabeth Williams

MY MUM

I love my mum,
Even though she sucks her thumb,
She's my best mum, my only mum,
But when I read her books in my head,
She turns the pages too fast,
But I still love her!

So I'm going to surprise her on Mother's Day,
With breakfast in bed and handmade presents,
She's the world's best mum,
Partly she rules
And she is an important part of my life and the family!

Taylor Baggott

The Best Mother

(Dedicated to all the mums in the world)

My mother is an amazing cook
And can guess our feelings with just a look.
She was the one who taught me how to read a book
And saved me when my life shook.

She is a nurse when I come home bleeding
And leads me when I need leading.
My mum helps me when I start pleading
And speeds me up when I need speeding.

She is a tailor when my dress needs a patch
And a designer when my clothes don't match.
My mum also taught me not to snatch
And will cry if I get just a little scratch.

She is my best friend
And is always there till the very end.
My mum straightens my life when it comes to a bend
And buys me things that are the current trend.

She plays with me and makes me share
And shows me that she'd always care.
My mother forgives me and says that I should be fair
But all that matters is that we make a perfect pair.

Thanisa Segar

EMERALD EYES

The day I met your emerald eyes,
Your entity lit my darkened skies.
You promised a gift of warmth and love
And have been a true blessing beyond and above.

You stand by my side through thick and thin
And conquer life, a true heroine.
A woman whose love injects my heart,
My long-life ally, never to part.

I can't describe my honest pride,
To have your presence in my life.
The joy you bring each trying day,
Striving to keep all worries at bay.

I seek inspiration from your life
And admire your lull of every strife.
Your unconditional earnest mind
And the extraordinary woman that you define.

We share a bond that links our souls,
A devotion of which makes us a whole.
Our love is one I can't disguise,
I'll forever be thankful for your emerald eyes.

Holly Amber Hope Thomas

Mummy Poem

M y mum is the best
U nder the cover of love
M y mum likes sleeping in the morning like me
M aybe she sleeps in her socks at night
Y es, I love her very much

P illow fights and cuddles galore
O h how I love her so
E very day she helps me get ready for school
M y mum is the best in the entire universe.

Jessica Lily Rae

MUMMY

I love my mum,
She can be so fun,
She looks after me
And my sister and daddy,
She never fails to come
When I need her,
My wonderful mum.

I love my mummy,
She is my best buddy,
When she gives me a hug,
My troubles go down the plug,
My mum is better than the rest,
She really, truly is the best,
I love my mum!

Victoria Miller

My Mum Is A...

(A Kennings Poem)

Care-giver
Food-cooker
Bath-runner
Tear-drier
Taxi-driver
Game-player
Hair-brusher
Homework-helper
Story-teller
House-cleaner
Bed-maker
Hoover-upper
Treat-buyer
Love-spreader.

Jessie-Jay Lola Barnes

TO MY MUM

To my mum who is always there
Who I love lots
No one else can compare

To my mum who always supports
Who is always here
She deserves a reward

To my mum who tries her best
Who works so hard
She barely rests

To my mum who thinks I'm great
Who loves me lots
And is my best mate

To my mum who is so tough
Like a firework full of love

Xx

Luci Louise Hill

YOU'RE A SUPER MUM

You're a super mum,
I'm a super son,
We can fly around the world,
You and me getting twirled.

You're a super mum,
I'm a super son,
We can go to Jupiter and Mars,
Look at the moon and stars.

You're a super mum,
I'm a super son,
We can travel to Paris and Mexico
And maybe even Texas, oh!

You're a super mum,
You do super things for me,
I hope I will always be a super son to you.

Oscar Burns (9)

LOVE LETTERS

(Dedicated to my Mum, Megan Kaspersen, Nana and Granny too)

Two letters, three letters, five letters,
A sentence that explains my feelings,
Two letters, three letters, five letters,
A sentence that keeps my heart reeling,
Two letters, three letters, five letters,
A statement that's totally true,
Two letters, three letters, five letters,
This is what I'm saying to you...
My mum rules!

Kiara Faye Kaspersen

WORLD'S BEST MUM

My mummy is the best,
Better than all the rest,
She is so sweet,
She gives me something to eat,
She has lovely eyes,
And she sings me lullabies,
She never kicks,
She is very quick,
She is very clean,
She is never mean,
She never bothers me
And she likes tea,
World's best mum.

Evie Busby (7)

My Wonderful Mum

Mum, all I can see when I wake up,
Is your love all around me.
Mum, you are so funny,
That I laugh every single day.
Mummy, you do never give up
And I would like to be as smart as you are.
I can't live without you,
You're so nice!
I love you so much.

Arthur Imankerdjo-Lambert

MY MUM IS THE BEST

Your hair shines like the dark sky,
I love your pretty, black, cat eyes.
I wonder who you are deep down inside,
I feel so lucky that you are my guide.

To my dad you make the perfect wife,
We are always together and you are in my life.
My mum is loving, kind and cunning,
She always goes for whatever challenge is coming.

She is a good listener and a great multitasker,
She is creative and deserves whatever she's after.
My mum can come in many forms,
But I'm okay however she's born.

Michaela Su San Maung

My Mummy

My mummy is best
My mummy is lovely
My mummy is great
My mummy is kind
My mummy is helpful
My mummy is happy
My mummy has loved me from when I was in her tummy!

Isla Rose Stewart

IRREPLACEABLE MOTHER

Mother, oh mother,
How strong and powerful you are.
Your relationship is unconditional, it's unforgettable.
Oh mother,
Your love for me is never ending,
I cherish every moment and it is memorable.

These worries you have never stop.
The world may seem to turn against you,
But your love remains the same.
Mother, my faith in you is eternal
And your teachings through every step of life are
phenomenal.
No one can replace you.

Your love is always there and I know you care.
Your words give me strength,
Whether it's in depth or length.
You bring me happiness and joy,
Even during hardships,
Or when I get annoyed.

You understand and comfort me however you can,
It always works
And I don't even need a cheese flan!
Your presence keeps my life going,
You make me succeed without knowing.
Oh, how can I say, I am fortunate to have a wonderful
mother like you.

Mother you are invaluable,
Irreplaceable,
I love you Mum.

Naima Sheema Anbia (12)

MY BEST CHUM

My mum, my mum,
Always glam but never glum,
My best chum, there is no one like my mum.
She takes me to school in a car and then says, "Ta-ra!"
My mum is worth all the gold,
She is really pretty but never old!

Eva Johal

MY BEAUTIFUL MUM

Mum, mum, oh how I love you!
I don't want someone new,
There isn't anyone better.
I can't thank you enough,
For everything you've done for me,
I just hope you can see,
You're the best mum ever!

Jake Barrett

Mummy, I Love You

Mummy, I love you because you brought me to this world,
Mummy, I love you because you help me when I am scared,
Mummy, I love you because you cook my favourite food,
Mummy, I love you because you help me with work,
Mummy, I love you because you take good care of me,
Mummy, I love you to the moon and stars and back.

Miqdad Mahmud

I LOVE MUMMY

I love mummy,
Her smile is warm and sunny,
Her kiss as sweet as honey.
I like spending her money,
I think she's very funny,
She's as cool as the Easter bunny.
She's just my mummy,
I love her!

Edward Taylor-Fullwood (6)

MY MUMMY'S THE BEST

My mummy's the best because she gives the best cuddles,
She takes me out and we jump in the puddles.
My mummy's the best, she gives the best kisses,
She always makes sure I get my wishes.

My mummy's the best because she loves me so much,
She always has the softest touch.
I love you mum, for being you,
I'm going to make you the very best brew!

Lily Eden

WORLD'S BEST MUM

A mum who cares for me
A mum with never-ending love for me
She'd sacrifice her life for me
For nine months she carried me.

She showed her love for me
She's my best friend and plays with me
When I'm in pain and sick, she makes me feel better
Who taught my infant lips to pray well.

Thanks for my mum who raises me up
You mean the world to me because of your love
Your love is enough for me no matter what!
Always there to support and prop me up.

To the greatest mum I've ever had
She's a strong woman and had a good heart
My sweet, loving mother and mentor
My adviser, my doctor and my tutor.

She loves me and protects me more than ever
A wonderful mum that loves me forever
No one can replace my love to her
My endless love, strength and mum forever.

Sunshinekate Pearce (6)

DEAR MUM

You've been there for summer
You've been there for winter
You've been there for me always
Even when it goes dark
Took me to the park
Through tough times
When you want to just give up
But you don't
You soldier on
You would chase me through the sun
And for that I thank you
I hope we stick together like glue
I love you too.

Alex Johns

Mum, You Shine Like The Sun!

To Mum, you shine like the sun,
When I am down, you pick me up off the ground,
When I frown, you put it under your crown
And that's why, out of all the mums in town,
My love for you abounds
And you are always around!

Alisha Taylor

MUM IS...

Mum is soft and gentle
Like a whisper in the wind
Mum is truly tender
I hope this never ends
You are like a river
Rambling on and on
Singing gently to me
Until you finish your song
I've a lot of love to give
That's why I love you.
Mum is like an angel
Heaven sent down to me
This angel gave me my eyes
So that clearly I can see
She gave me my hands
So that I can feel and touch
The angel that's with me all my life
Who I love so much
I've a lot of love to give
That's why I love you.

Sybil Somerset (17)

MY MUM

My mum is the best
She is better than the rest
She always makes me tea
And gives me peas
I love my mum
She is so much fun
Whenever I need her
She is always there.

Charlotte H S Salt

FAVOURITE MUM

My mum is one of a kind
My mum's favourite animal is a sheep
My mum is amazing
My favourite mum is fun
My favourite mum took me sledging last week
My favourite mum is cool
My lovely mum helps me with my homework
My lovely mum helps my grandad at lambing time
My lovely mum makes me and my fun sister yummy teas
My lovely mum takes us out with my really fun and amazing
grandma
And my mum works hard
My mum is lucky to have me!

Katie Balderson

FABULOUS MUM

F antastically amazing, she's my mum
A mazingly delightful, she's my mum
B eautifully presented, she's my mum
U tterly loud and proud, she's my mum
L usciously sweet and soft, she's my mum
O utrageously comical, she's my mum
U sing glitter and sparkles, she's my mum
S melling gorgeous, she's my mum

M um, you are my superstar
U p so high, so magical
M oments we share together, I'm so glad you're my mum.

Eliyah Irene Schwartz

MY MOM IS MY HOPE AND BEST FRIEND

The warmth of her hug, the care in her smile,
The encouragement to keep laughing,
The energy to keep loving.

A rose does not bloom without sunshine,
A root does not grow without earth,
A seed does not sprout without soil.

A mother's love is the sunlight to the flowers standing tall in the field,
The nourishment to blossom and shine every day.
Thank you Mum, you allowed me to prosper.

Samsam Adam Ali

MOTHER

M is for memories we make together
O is for others you always put first
T is for the best mam ever
H is for the hugs I love the most
E is for everything you do for me
R is for reassuring me that I can do my best.

I love my mam!

Lillie Mae Burke

A Smiling Flower

Mum, whatever mood you're in,
You'll still be in the drops of love showing kindness,
You show cooperation and show humility,
Because you are the most loving mum.
You are a smiling flower
And you are happy Harriot.

Deen Musundire

WHAT A MUM MEANS TO ME

My mum is always there
She's ready in mid-air
Up and down the stairs
She is always there

Cooking breakfast, lunch and dinner
Washing up
She's a winner
Cleaning with us day by day
It's the main thing of the day

A mum is more than one thing after all
A loving person and lots more
Laughing, loving, caring, that's not all
Mum, mummy, mother
They're all the same with a friendly smile through the day.

Sarah Rodriguez

Teacher

She crossed borders so I wouldn't have to,
She learnt this language from anew.
She works and works and still keeps working
And to herself she stays true.
She teaches me to be content,
With what I have and what I don't.
She says to stop at satisfaction,
To keep my smile and never moan.

She says it's the life we're in where things aren't fair,
Where judgements sit and people stare.
It's a world where those like to put their nose,
In places they don't belong.
So count your blessings child,
It's a wild world out there.
Don't listen to the gossip and don't be the one to gossip
And what you have, remember to share.

Mum, my guidance, my rock.
Thank you for teaching me not to change for anyone.
To work hard and be resilient,
To do things right and learn from the wrong.
Thank you for letting me know of the others less fortunate,
For teaching me how to make my way through the crowd.
Thank you for opening up the world to me,
I promise I will make you proud.

Sela Musa

MY MUM

My mum is my life,
My mum catches me when I fall,
My mum holds me when I am down,
My mum is very special,
My mum is lovely and gorgeous on the outside,
But on the inside my mum is very unique,
My mum holds an important place in my heart,
Where would I be without my mum?
My mum is my life.

Hafsah Mehmood

MUM

Like a star, you're the shiniest in the sky
Like a chef, you make a brilliant pie
Like a nurse, you look after me
Like an entertainer, you take me to the sea
Like an astronaut, you're daring
Like a teacher, you're encouraging
Like a bird, you love to sing
(Even though it can be embarrassing)
You buy me magazines
You deserve a limousine
And that's why I love you so, so much.

Sophie Williams

WORLD'S BEST MUM

You always seem to know what's wrong,
Before I have to say,
You seem to know what's on my mind,
If I'm feeling down that day.

I never have to ask for help,
You're always there to guide me.
If at times I need support,
You're always right beside me.

You've been my rock throughout my life,
Wanting nothing in return.
You've made me who I am today,
Helping me to grow and learn.

Thank you will never be enough,
For everything you've done.
You're my friend, my angel, my guardian
And, most importantly,
The world's best mum.

Aleshia Burt (11)

The World's Best Mum, Is My Mum

I love my mum,
These are the reasons why!
She cleans up my mess,
She helps me to prepare my tests at school,
My mum gives me love, she gives me cuddles
And she cares, she helps with my hair,
She gets all the knots out of my hair.
Together we have so much in common
And sometimes we share nearly everything.
She's my mum, my world,
We even have a special blood type that we share because it's rare.
Christmas and birthdays are special too,
My mum gets me what I want without me even having to say,
My mum surprises me, I love surprises,
I love my mum.
I love my mum even when she's in a mood,
Because I always give her big hugs and kisses.
I tell her I love her to the moon and back,
I always put a smile on her face,
Because Mum, I love you, I really do,
You're my world, I love you, I really do,
Because you're the greatest mum in the world.
That I know is true so thanks Mum for being the best mum in the world,
So I'll love you always and forever.

Codie Jane Moore (10)

MUMMY

My mummy is there when I'm in despair!
I love my mummy.
I wake up in the morning,
She means my life's not boring!
My mummy helps me for the future,
But I love her more than that!
I look up to her,
She is my hero,
Who helps me when I'm down,
Or when I've got a frown!
My mummy is not just family,
My mummy is my friend.
Love, nothing can beat.
With love you have no need for greed!
Love is a spark that turns you into fire,
That will guide you to success!
Love can beat greed!
Greed is the night, love is the day!
My love is for my mummy,
She is my spark!

Ben Chirstopher Millard

GRATEFUL

Mummy you are the best mum in the world,
You make me happy
And when I am sad you make me laugh,
Ha ha ha!

Mummy you are the best mum in the world,
You help me with everything,
You are grateful for who you are
And you love everybody.

Mummy you are the best mum in the world.
All your friends love you
because you're always happy, thankful and friendly.
Mummy you are the best mum in the whole entire world.
Love you!

Ffion Hurley

WORLD'S BEST MUM

My mum who is my dad's wife,
My mum who has big and brown eyes,
My mum who has long black-brown hair,
My mum who has peach skin with small brown spots,
My mum who has two holes in her ears so she can put some beautiful earrings on.
My mum who has magic hands to make different types of cakes,
Like a Superman cake, a car cake and lots more cakes.
My mum who goes to college to learn to be a nurse.
I love my mum because she is learning and working hard.
I love my mum because she is pretty.
I love my mum because I always have a wonderful time with her.
I think my mum is the best mum in the whole wide world.
I hope your mum is like this too!

Haozhe Weng

MY MUM IS THE WORLD TO ME

My mum's the world to me,
This is for you Mum,
Roses are red,
Violets are blue,
I've written a song, just for you!
Here's some pretty flowers and cards,
From the people you love and who love you!
You'll always be my mum
And we'll always celebrate Mother's Day for you,
My mum doesn't just care for me,
She cares for others too.
She'll always help me in hard times, I know it.
My beautiful mum lightens up the world for me!
That's my mum for sure!

Laaibah Hussain (10)

My Beautiful Mum

Do you remember when we first met?
I was snuggled up in my nice warm bed.
Got home for my first ever night,
Slept like an angel and snuggled up tight.
I hope you remember, my beautiful mum,
You know, the day I became your son.
Your glory and love fill the house,
Moving around as quiet as a mouse,
But of course I know that it's there,
A mum like you is very rare.
I could say much more but for now,
I love you.
Who loves you the most?
I do!

Georgie Southon

WHY I LOVE MY MUM!

I love my mum because
She cooks me dinner every night,
And she held my hand on my first flight.

I love my mum because,
She gets me medicine when I'm unwell,
And she once let me ring her 'Prosecco bell'.

I love my mum because,
I can go to the park on my own,
And I once chewed her left over chicken bone!

I love my mum because,
She lets me sleep with her in bed,
She always makes sure I've read.
I love my mum because she's perfect!

Isobel Moody

OH MY MUMMY

Oh my mummy
You look brighter than the sun
Oh my mummy
Wow! You're very fun
When I'm in bed
She sees me curl up
And thinks "Aw!"
And gives me a hug
Oh my mummy
I see you everywhere
Oh my mummy
You're like my fairy godmother
No one loves you more than me.

Nicolé Howley

THE HUGE LOVE

My mama is special
Her skin is so soft
She gives me lots of cuddles
I love her a lot!

My mama is special
She reads me lots of books
I love her so very much
When she cooks.

My mama is special
She does great things for me
I love her so much
When she drinks her tea.

My mama is special
I love it when we laugh and giggle
When she tickles me
I wriggle and jiggle.

I love her so much!
I love her so much!

Chiara Bonici-Mompalao-Lee

MY LOVELY MOTHER

My mum is brave, my mum is kind
She helps me even in the hardest times
When I am all alone, sad and scared
She will come to the rescue and make me glad
I love my mum, she is just so great
That is why she is the... best.

Karina Sood

My Mum

My mum does my homework with me,
My mum helps me,
My mum spends time with me,
My mum looks after me,
My mum is special,
My mum is kind,
My mum has good ideas,
My mum loves me and I love her too.

Nicolette Panteli

My Mother

My mother is sweet,
She makes my heart beat
And she loves tiramisu!
She picks me up from school,
It is like she has been in the pool.
Her smile grows from ear to ear,
You should see her cheer and cheer!

It is Mother's Day at last
And I say, "I love you," and she says she loves me,
It is the best relationship there can be.

Sofia Louisa Lenior-Emanuel

TO THE WORLD'S BEST MUM

I know I've got in trouble for laughing at your bum,
I know you know my secrets, I suck my thumb,
But what can I say, we all are dumb,
I know I'm unfair, I know I don't share,
But my love for you is beyond compare,
Going swimming for leisure,
Spending time with you is such a pleasure,
It's better than gold, better than treasure,
You're my role model, you're my number one,
You are so much fun, you can be lazy,
Overall you're sweet and kind, like a summer's daisy,
I wrote this poem to say thank you,
For everything you do,
I love you.

Aisha Ali (12)

I LOVE YOU MUM...

You're caring,
You're daring,
You're forgiving,
Always giving,
You're kind,
One of a kind,
A great cook,
You love books,
Happy day and night,
You make my life bright!

Reon Dhir

TO THE WORLD'S BEST MUM

(For putting up with my bad jokes!)

Life is hard,
But love is not
And I do
Love you a lot.
I really hope
You love me too,
As sure as
A cow goes moo.

Fern Margetson

MAGIC MUM

M agic,
U nforgettable
M um.

I always know when you're around,
Because everyone smiles from all around,
When someone starts crying about something sad,
Suddenly Mum appears and she puts a plaster on
And off she goes because she's my magic mum.

Hannah Corley

Super Mum

Who cleaned my room and tidied my books?
Who made the dinner and cleaned the dishes?
Who signed my homework diary and packed my woolly hat?
I wonder who does all of these things?
I wake up early the next day looking for this mysterious
hero,
I hear someone downstairs,
I went to take a look,
I couldn't believe it, it was my mum!
She was signing my homework diary!
I knew it was her.
She really is my super mum.

Haarith Hanif Bapu

MY MUM POEM

My mum smells of candy and sunshine
But so fluffy and cute.
Her hair is carpet fluffy.
She loves to go out and about.
My mum loves the songs I do.
She has a coat that is silky like her heart.
My mum loves going to the Co-op to get the deals.
My mum loves her cups of tea,
Especially if they're made by Daddy.
She has coffee sometimes.
My mum loves multicoloured sunglasses,
Which make her look cool.
She's my top mum and I wouldn't change her for anyone
And that's my mum, she's my number one.

Shannan Harvey-Bullock

Young Writers Information

We hope you have enjoyed reading this book – and that you will continue to in the coming years.

If you're a young writer who enjoys reading and creative writing, or the parent of an enthusiastic poet or story writer, do visit our website www.youngwriters.co.uk. Here you will find free competitions, workshops and games, as well as recommended reads, a poetry glossary and our blog.

If you would like to order further copies of this book, or any of our other titles give us a call or visit www.youngwriters.co.uk.

Young Writers
Remus House
Coltsfoot Drive
Peterborough
PE2 9BF

(01733) 890066
info@youngwriters.co.uk